The Seeing Transformation

Bruce Lindley

Foreword by Patricia King

The Seeing Transformation
by Bruce Lindley
Copyright © 2015 Bruce Lindley

Published by
Australian Apostolic Restore Community (A.A.R.C.)
PO Box 3493
Helensvale B.C. QLD 4212
Australia

This book or parts thereof may not be reproduced in any form, stored in a retrieval system, or transmitted in any form by any means – electronic, mechanical, photocopy, recording or otherwise – without prior written permission of the publisher, except as provided by Australian copyright law.

All Scripture quotations are from the New International Version 2011 of the Bible unless otherwise specified.

Scripture taken from the HOLY BIBLE, NEW INTERNATIONAL VERSION. Copyright © 2011 by Zondervan. Used by permission of Zondervan. All rights reserved.

Cover design by Fiverr and Rachel Lindley

ISBN: 978-0-9942402-0-0

Printed in United States of America
For Worldwide Distribution

Dedication

The Seeing Transformation is dedicated to my Heavenly Father who continues to allow me to live in new levels of "seeing" in the spiritual realm. Thank You for opening my eyes to see. You are the most amazing Father.

This is also dedicated to my precious wife Cheryl whose passion and intimacy with Jesus inspires and challenges me to new depths of encountering God, and to my wonderful children whose hunger for more and more of Him causes me to be a blessed dad.

Acknowledgements

This book wouldn't have been possible without the support and help of Cheryl Lindley and her ongoing commitment, love and input into this project.

A special thank you, Patricia King and our XP Ministries family, for your love and encouragement. May you continue to reap a great harvest of changed lives.

Special thanks to Carol Martinez for her advice and wonderful editing skills.

Contents

Foreword – Patricia King   7

Introduction – Get Ready to See   9

Chapter 1 – Looking Inside Out   13

Chapter 2 – A New Season of Seeing   21

Chapter 3 – Learning to See Yourself with God's Eyes   31

Chapter 4 – Unlocking Your Seeing to Live in the Miraculous   51

Chapter 5 – Wrong Seeing   67

Chapter 6 – Unlocking the Things that Stop Your Seeing   75

Chapter 7 – Seeing with Kingdom Eyes - Part 1   89

Chapter 8 – Seeing with Kingdom Eyes - Part 2   101

Final Encouragement – What I See for You   113

Endnotes   115

Australian Apostolic Resource Community

Additional Resources by Bruce Lindley

Contact

Foreword

Patricia King

There are appointed times in history when God highlights specific aspects of His nature, abilities, power, and wisdom. In this season, the "seer anointing" is being highlighted by the Spirit of Grace.

An awesome invitation from God Himself is being given to you. Would you like to grow in your ability to see as God sees? Jesus said, "I only do the things I see My Father do" (John 5:19). Seeing is important! Jesus was very aware of that when He lived in the earth, and today it is vital for us to live with God's perspective and vision as the world lives in confusion and turmoil.

Abraham saw his generations of descendants when he did not have even one child yet. Joseph saw solutions that preserved both Egypt and his own people. Esther saw a victory for her people in a critical hour of assault. Daniel saw things to come in the last days. John the Baptist saw the true identity of Jesus as the Christ in the waters of baptism. Jesus saw a multitude being fed when there were only a few loaves of bread and a couple of fish in His hands. All these great men and women of faith saw with God's vision and perspective and as a result acted on His behalf, giving Him glory. You are also called to be in such a company of seers.

Bruce Lindley enthusiastically shares revelation regarding *The Seeing Transformation*. Your life can be transformed by the way you see, the way you perceive. Jesus taught that to enter the Kingdom, you must enter like a child, and Bruce certainly stirred childlike faith and excitement in me when I read this inspiring book.

As you read this book, may you receive an impartation of faith, revelation, and anointing in the realm of God-perception and vision. I believe that this book could be your doorway into a brand new realm of discovery in anointed and fulfilled Kingdom life.

Introduction

Get Ready to See

It is time for a SEEING transformation! If you change the way you SEE, everything will change; your life will be transformed into a completely new way of living.

To SEE means "to perceive with the eyes, to perceive mentally, to discern, understand, to visualize."[1]

Since my wife and I have changed the way we SEE, remarkable miracles and spectacular victories have broken out in our lives. A week does not go by without seeing a completely impossible situation become a reality.

These things do not happen because God treats us differently than anyone else. He will do the same for you if you change the way you see!

You have an opportunity to see God work in your life in a way you have never experienced before! Your life will be impacted for good. In fact, you can be transformed in the way you see God, the way you see yourself, the way you see others and even the way you see the world.

You can experience a "seeing transformation"!

This is the season of seeing remarkable miracles on a new level.

Miracles will begin to happen when you change the way you see.

Even though my wife Cheryl and I had already experienced a level of miracles for a number of years, a new realm of even more frequent and remarkable miracles began for us in the United States in August 2014 when I heard Shawn Bolz speak at our H.I.M. international conference[2] in Pasadena. He shared how several years ago he received a call from Jill Austin very late at night asking him to come over to her house, as a miraculous anointing from God was visiting her. She had been reading about the life of the late Ruth Heflin and felt God was transferring her mantle to the next generation of young preachers. Shawn immediately organized other friends to come with him to Jill's home. God's presence was so strong that they prayed together for over nine hours while remarkable Spirit-occurences took place in each individual. Ruth Heflin's mantle was not just for one person but transferrable to many.

That day in Pasadena, Shawn Bolz, through the powerful revelation of the Holy Spirit, called out names and birthdays of people, and even the names of their spouses. It was with life transforming-purpose as a new level of SEEING had become accessible to all of us! And it came on me.

As a result the whole atmosphere changed in the room. I experienced my own SEEING TRANSFORMATION that day. I started to see revelation about the lives of every person I looked at that day. Now whenever I step out to receive in faith, the same operation of the Spirit manifests.

The Spirit has released a SEEING TRANSFORMATION into the earth right now! We have been prophetically proclaiming its coming for some time, but now we are actually experiencing it in accelerated levels.

The prophet Isaiah saw it a long time ago when he prophesied what God has available for every believer. In Isaiah 43:19 he decrees,

"SEE, I am doing a new thing!

Now it springs up; do you not [SEE] it?

I am making a way in the wilderness and streams in the wasteland." (uppercase added)

A new level of SEEING REMARKABLE MIRACLES has become accessible to you, too!

This book reveals how God has always intended for you to SEE. Rather than allowing circumstances, your upbringing, your own emotions or other people's attitudes and actions to affect the way you see life, God has another way of seeing, just for you.

Today you are about to learn how to unlock your "seeing" so remarkable miracles will become your everyday reality. This grace from God will change the way you perceive, speak and live.

Are you ready to SEE your life transformed?

Then get ready to SEE like you have never seen before!

CHAPTER 1

Looking Inside Out

Our home is a little different than most homes in Australia: we have a house of prayer in our garage. Instead of having cars there, we have carpet, chairs, a piano, banners and a map of the world on the wall. Our garage is where we meet with God, and people like to come and join us to pray. My wife Cheryl spends a lot of her life in our house of prayer. Each Friday a number of local leaders join us. One of our team recently had a great spiritual vision of a cloud of witnesses overlooking us all. Then he saw me pick up cannon balls of joy, insert them into a cannon and then shoot the anointed cannon balls of joy into a crowd of Christians in a church I was to speak at the following weekend. As he spoke out the vision, I saw it in my mind's eye also.

The following Sunday, as I shared this vision the congregation started to shout and laugh, sensing God's presence and a new joy and freedom. Now as I just described that to you, you may have begun to see the impression of it also, just like I did when I first heard my team member share it.

You might try to explain that is just a person's imagination at work. The imagination is so often downplayed by many believers. They think that if a vision or impression is seen in the imagination, then it cannot be from God. This thinking is naïve. God created our imagination so that we could experience vision, just like Him. Any type of vision you receive from God will in some way be connected to the imagination – after all, you do not receive a vision in your big toe or your liver! No, the imagination is that part of us that hosts and fosters vision.

The issue is the source. Where does the vision come from? Vision can be sourced in our own carnal nature or even from a demonic temptation, but God's visions line up with His character, nature, and Word. His visions bear the fruit of the Spirit. In this case, every time I share that picture with people, they experience dimensions of God's joy – some even start to laugh and shout for joy, too. Why? Because, like me, they see it happening to themselves also!

Romans 14:17 says:

> For the kingdom of God is not a matter of eating and drinking, but of righteousness, peace and joy in the Holy Spirit.

If you do not have joy in your life, then one third of the kingdom of God is missing in you! It IS possible to live in this joy! You just have to change the way you see your life – seeing it from God's perspective.

If you need some joy, I release a joy explosion right now in you. What you see will become a reality for you! Now if you don't see anything right now – hang on, just be patient. God is going to unlock your seeing for you, too.

So many Christians struggle in life with season after season of discouragement and unanswered prayer. As a result, many even change what they believe, or lower their faith expectation so they won't be disappointed or frustrated anymore. God does not want us to live this way! He wants us to see life through His lens. And as our seeing is lined up with His truth, we will experience His goodness and promises.

> AS OUR SEEING IS LINED UP WITH GOD'S TRUTH, WE WILL EXPERIENCE HIS GOODNESS AND PROMISES.

THE POWER OF CHRIST'S RESURRECTION WITHIN YOU

Many believers don't truly know who and what is inside us. Romans 8:11 says,

> The [same] spirit of Him that raised Christ from the dead dwells in you.

Dwells where? Inside us! This resurrection power is living inside you. The most wonderful lifestyle you can ever have is when you live in the resurrection power of Christ that is already inside you. This is the promise that Jesus gave to all disciples, and this includes you.

Acts 1:8 says,

> But you will receive power when the Holy Spirit comes on you; and you will be my witnesses in Jerusalem, and in all Judea and Samaria, and to the ends of the earth.

That word *power* is translated from the Greek word "dunamis."[1] That is the same word as for dynamite and it refers to God's miracle-working power. You have explosive power inside you. The truth is, you and I are dangerous to the enemy and his schemes. But sadly I have discovered that most Christians don't know who and what is truly inside them.

How can I be sure of that? It is because most Christians don't manifest this type of miracle-working power.

I have been in ministry for over thirty years, but I am just now experiencing the manifestation of signs and wonders in great increase because I have received a new perception or way of seeing. Paul calls this "the eyes of our understanding" in Ephesians 1:18. When your perception changes, so will your life.

Living in the supernatural power of the Spirit has become normal lifestyle for me now, and you can live this way too! It is for every believer – not just for a select few. I want to encourage you today.

We are encountering new levels of glory and it is available to you. God truly desires this for you!

Second Corinthians 3:17–18 (NIV) says,

> Now the Lord is the Spirit, and where the Spirit of the Lord is, there is freedom. And we all, who with unveiled faces contemplate the Lord's glory, are being transformed into his image with ever-increasing glory, which comes from the Lord, who is the Spirit.

There is more for you today – a whole new level. Don't be satisfied with your current status of spiritual experience. There is more, and it is freely available for you!

We travel to Africa twice a year and minister in leadership events regarding the apostolic reformation.[2] Recently while we were in Uganda a lady approached me and asked, "Do you remember me?" Because we pray for so many people, I don't often remember. She said I had prayed for her a year ago because she had AIDS, and that when I prayed, nothing happened. Statements like hers no longer intimidate me.

> LIVING IN THE SUPERNATURAL POWER OF THE HOLY SPIRIT CAN BE THE LIFESTYLE FOR EVERY BELIEVER – NOT JUST FOR A SELECT FEW.

Why? When you realize it is the Holy Spirit's responsibility and not yours to heal, it takes all the pressure from you. It sets you free to be conduits or vehicles of the Holy Spirit's power.

It turned out that even though nothing happened immediately, after a few days she said her body began to feel different. Every three months she was required to go for a checkup at the AIDS clinic to see if the disease had progressed. So she went and got tested. The medical personnel checking her results advised her that there was something wrong with the test because they couldn't find the AIDS virus, so they tested her again the same day. It was the same result. No AIDS! They told her something must be wrong with the whole batch of tests, so they told her to come back the next week.

She went back the next week and the result was the same – no AIDS virus present in her body! She informed me that she returned monthly for six months with the same results each time. They finally told her that they didn't want to see her any more, as she was completely healed!

Now I want to encourage you. I don't have some unique healing gift. I am just like you. You have the same resurrection power inside you, and this is normal Christian living.

All you have to do is to choose to believe what Jesus said in Luke 9:1 when He said He gave his disciples authority to heal the sick and the cast out demons.

Mark 16:17 says,

These signs shall accompany those who believe.

Do not be an unbelieving believer. You are created to be a believing believer. You have authority to heal the sick and cast out demons. This is your normal Christian life.

You can learn more on how to naturally live a supernatural life in my book, *Encountering the Supernatural*.[3]

INSIDE OUT

Most people live life looking through their natural eyes. But God does not want you to look from the outside in. He wants you to look from the inside out! From the real you – your spirit!

Second Corinthians 5:17 reveals that when you are born again, your old way of living has gone and you step into a new way of living. So you should spend your time looking after the most valuable part of you – your spiritual man.

The key is to realize how important, how valuable this part of your life is to you. Once you do, you will move to another realm of spiritual life. This becomes the part of your life that you give the most time, energy and attention into building, as you begin to live through this new way of seeing.

Paul says it is good to look after our physical being but it is even better to look after our spiritual being. Your spiritual well-being won't ever change until you change your spiritual seeing.

Begin to see from the inside out!

CHAPTER 2

A New Season of Seeing

There has been a change in season for all believers! It is not just a nondescript new season of change. It is a season in which we SEE things shift quickly and powerfully.

God gave Cheryl and me a powerful personal encounter in June 2013 as the means for us to begin to SEE the shift that accompanied this new season.

That day we were in our house of prayer and had just finished a "prayer set," which normally lasts for one or two hours. As I was walking out the door to go to a meeting, I suddenly stopped. It was as if someone had hit me in the stomach. One moment I was walking and the next moment I was stopped in my tracks. I turned to my wife and said,

"*Something has just shifted!*" I didn't know what had happened but I just knew that something had changed! Something had shifted in the Spirit – it was a new season. I heard the Lord say, "*The old has gone – the new has come.*"

That night, June 27, 2013, the prime minister of our nation was overthrown. In Australia we don't have a presidential system, but rather a parliamentary system in which our elected politicians vote to decide who will become prime minister. That night our government leaders removed the existing prime minister and elected a new one.

Then later that same week, there was an uprising in Egypt and President Mubarak was overthrown. That really got my attention. Up until then I had thought this shift or change of seasons was personal. Now I realized it was more than that. The international and national changes were natural signs of what had taken place in the spirit realm.

It is what God is doing across the world in the body of Christ. Hallelujah! It's a new day!

"See, I am doing a new thing!"

Isaiah the prophet saw it, too. He saw it in his day but he also looked forward into the future and saw it for today.

When does it spring up? NOW!

For many years I have been praying and declaring that revival would come to our nation. Now I have stopped saying "revival is coming" because I have changed the way I see.

Chapter 2: A New Season of Seeing

> Isaiah 43:19 says (repeat it out loud),
> "SEE, I AM DOING A NEW THING!
> NOW IT SPRINGS UP..."

I now *see* with the eyes of revival. Rather than seeing what still has to happen, I see in faith that revival has already become a reality. If you can *see* with His eyes, you will see that it is already here! If you can't see revival, it means you are not looking with God's eyes.

We need to begin to SEE with GOD'S EYES!

"NOW it springs up; do you not perceive it?"

If you do not perceive or see what is happening with your spiritual eyes, it is possible that revival is happening all around you but you are missing it!

There are so many examples of people praying for revival, then missing it because it came in a way that they did not expect or perceive it would come.

The Azusa Street Pentecostal Revival in 1906 is the classic example. A group of leaders in Los Angeles were praying and believing for the same manifestation of revival that was taking place in Wales, known as the Welsh Revival, in which thousands turned to God, transforming their land. These church leaders wanted the same revival outpouring to come to Los Angeles, but their prayers were answered in a way that they did not expect.

Instead, God sent an African American from Oklahoma named William Seymour to Los Angeles. When the leadership invited him to their church, he preached a passionate revival message, but it included a teaching many did not like – the baptism of the Holy Spirit accompanied by speaking in tongues.

Those who had been praying for revival could not *see* or "perceive" that this was God's answer to their prayers. So that night they locked the revival and William Seymour out of their church when he returned to speak as scheduled. The very thing that they had been praying for, they rejected, because it didn't come packaged in the way they expected. They were bound by traditional perception or seeing, expectations and past experience, and could not perceive it spiritually. Seymour then began ministering at a small prayer group on Bonnie Brae Street that was able to *see* what God was doing, and the world was forever changed.

Just because God moved in a certain way in your life in the past does not mean He will work that way in the future! I want to challenge you to be willing to change your perception.

> Decree with me:
>
> "I AM GOING TO CHANGE THE WAY I SEE TODAY."

SEE IT WITH YOUR "FAITH EYES."

Hebrews 11:1 (NKJV) declares,

Chapter 2: A New Season of Seeing

Now faith is the substance of things hoped for, the evidence of things not seen.

What you see will become your reality. But you have to see it in your spirit first!

One of the best examples of this was a young blind girl I met in Mombasa, Kenya, in 2010. We were holding a village crusade at dusk. The worship was amazing! All the young people were moving in unison. No one was telling them to all move to the left or to the right at the same time – they instinctively knew which way to go. I will tell you I couldn't follow them – this white man can't dance!

While they worshipped and danced, I noticed a very sad-looking young woman, about 16 years old, holding onto a tree. I went over and asked her why she looked so sad and was not dancing with her friends.

She said, *"I am blind, I cannot see."*

Then I asked, "Do you believe that Jesus will heal you?"

Notice I didn't say, "Do you believe that Jesus CAN heal you?," rather, "Do you believe that Jesus WILL heal you?"

She answered with an emphatic "Yes!"

So I prayed, "Lord, according to her faith, in the name of Jesus I release healing." She screamed out, "I can see!" Her eyes were instantly healed and she saw!

The first thing she did was to run over and join her friends who were dancing to the vibrant worship.

The truth is that she SAW in her spirit long before she saw naturally.

This is exactly what I am saying needs to take place in our lives, too, so we can have a seeing transformation!

A spirit of refreshing…

As I was praying about this need, I heard the Lord say,

"The majority of Christians have been taught how to live in the spirit realm, but many have battle fatigue."

In this new season, the Lord has released a spirit of refreshing that can change your mindset, causing you to refocus and see with a clarity you've never experienced before, in Jesus' name.

SEE … AND BE AMAZED!

How we see and what we see impacts and affects our lives.

It also impacts others, cities, cultures and nations. Oh, how we need to see with God's eyes so that we may bring life that will transform them!

> I invite you to pray this prayer now:
>
> "LORD, I NEED A NEW ANOINTING TO SEE WITH SPIRITUAL EYES! I ASK THAT YOU RELEASE A WHOLE NEW REALM OF SPIRITUAL SEEING TO ME NOW, IN THE NAME OF JESUS."

A classic example of the need to SEE with God's eyes was Moses. Moses had a powerful supernatural encounter with God in which God called him to be the deliverer of the people of Israel. When he finally agreed to, and obeyed, the king of Egypt refused to comply with Moses' demands. In fact, Pharaoh reacted badly to Moses and oppressed his people even more.

We will discuss this further in the next chapter. However, ultimately Moses had to stop seeing with his natural eyes and begin to see with God's eyes. It was and still is the only way to get through an impossible situation.

Each one of us has to make this same decision when we are facing an impossible situation.

How are we going to look at the situation – as possible or impossible? If you see it as impossible, you will see it through your eyes and not through God's eyes.

"With men this is impossible, but with God ALL things are possible."

He also said in Mark 9:23,

"ALL things are possible to him who believes."

So you have a choice!

If you determine to see through the eyes of God, then you have to BELIEVE! And when you believe, then you SEE!!!

See ... and listen!

The good news is that God is not intimidated by how impossible your circumstances may look.

One of the ways I learned to step into the realm of the supernatural was through my holy imagination.

Genesis 1:26 tells us,

God made mankind in HIS image, in HIS likeness.

When God made you in His image, He also created your imagination, as we discussed in chapter one. Since God created it, your imagination is not naturally evil. You can choose to have a sanctified – a holy – imagination. Make this your choice and see!

> As a practical aid, try closing your eyes and use your holy sanctified imagination to pull back the curtain of the natural. Step into the supernatural and begin to see with spiritual eyes.
>
> What do you see? _____
> _____
> _____
> _____

When I first began to do this, I only saw the back of my eyelids!

But I soon discovered that spending time in worship and praying in tongues helped me to focus on listening for God's voice. Then I would begin to sense the presence of the Holy Spirit.

I learned to ask God questions such as, "What are You saying to people here today?" Then I would stop and listen. Slowly I began to hear phrases like, "Tell them I have got them," or "Tell them not to be afraid and to trust Me."

Then I would ask God questions regarding specific people: "Who is your anointing on? What is their destiny? Do you have anything to say to them?"

This is how I learned how to give words of knowledge and prophecy over people.

But then I realized I could go still further into the realm of seeing in the Spirit!

I started to look for God's presence in the room. I asked more questions, such as,

"Are there any angels here? What type of anointing is here and how do You want me to flow with it?" I would use my holy imagination to look and see!

In the process, I learned how to discern God's voice and see clearly what God was doing in meetings.

I realized that one doesn't have to be in a church setting and worship for at least thirty minutes in order to experience this. I began to live like this every day. You too can live like this ALL the time!

THIS IS THE SEASON FOR A WHOLE NEW WAY OF SEEING! You do not have to wait any longer! You can start to see NOW!

CHAPTER 3

Learning to See Yourself with God's Eyes

Every day we make a choice. You can look at your life through the eyes of your circumstances or you can look at your life the way God sees you. Which lens are you going to use – the lens of circumstances that shout "impossible to overcome" or through God's lens?

Abraham had that choice. The Bible tells us that God had given Abraham a promise; he was going to be the father of many nations. But he had a problem – both he and his wife Sarah were barren. The facts said that it was impossible for them to have children. But in God nothing is impossible – Abraham and Sarah needed to change the way they "saw" in order to see that the impossible was indeed possible.

What did Abraham do?

Romans 4:19–21 says,

> Without weakening in his faith, he faced the fact that his body was as good as dead – since he was about a hundred years old – and that Sarah's womb was also dead. Yet he did not waver through unbelief regarding the promise of God, but was strengthened in his faith and gave glory to God, being fully persuaded that God had power to do what he had promised.

Both the truth of God's promise and the facts of Abraham's circumstances were real. He had to make a decision. He could believe either the facts or the truth as his reality!

The Bible tells us that Abraham believed God's promise because he was *fully persuaded* that God's promise was more of a reality than the facts. He believed that the impossible was more than possible – it was his reality.

How do you learn to live like this?

The answer is that you need to LEARN to SEE with GOD'S EYES. Seeing is a matter of perspective. Think about that for a moment.

Your perspective affects your whole outlook on life. Your priorities – beginning with where you have placed God on that "list" – your family, finances, leisure and others impact how you live today.

Unfortunately, most people spend their lives choosing, reacting, coping and changing in response to what happens

> ABRAHAM BELIEVED GOD'S
> PROMISE BECAUSE HE WAS FULLY
> PERSUADED THAT GOD'S PROMISE
> WAS MORE OF A REALITY
> THAN THE FACTS.

to them, instead of becoming actively involved in determining the course of their lives.

Today you have a new choice!

Either we can choose God's perspective or we can allow our circumstances to color the way we see.

THE MOSES PRINCIPLE

As we mentioned in the previous chapter, God called Moses to be His deliverer of the people of Israel, and he finally agreed. But Moses had a problem; when he delivered God's message to Pharaoh, Pharaoh refused to comply.

It gets worse for Moses according to Exodus 6:9,

> Moses reported this to the Israelites, but they did not listen to him because of their discouragement and harsh labor.

God's people stopped listening to Moses because of their discouragement.

Discouragement is one of the greatest weapons against our ability to see with God's eyes. We cannot have God's perspective if we allow discouragement to fill our seeing.

Discouragement causes more people to give up on their God-destiny than anything else. This and the reality of their circumstances stole all faith and hope out of the Israelites' hearts, and it will do the same for us if we let it!

Moses needed to SEE with God's eyes instead. It was the only way through an impossible situation. But God is the God of the impossible!

You need to make a choice.

What are you going to look at, your circumstances or God's promise?

You have to choose between them: in faith doing everything God tells you to do, or allowing your seemingly impossible circumstances to dominate your thinking and your future.

God's way of seeing

The truth is that you need God's perspective. What does God's way of seeing look like?

Look at what God says to Moses in Exodus 7:1,

> Then the Lord said to Moses, "SEE, I have made you like God to Pharaoh."

This is an amazing statement! *What* did God say to Moses?

"SEE, I have made you LIKE GOD."

In other words, God was telling Moses to begin to *SEE himself the way God saw him.*

Chapter 3: Learning to See with God's Eyes

God was saying to Moses, "You have been seeing with your natural eyes and you have been dominated by your circumstances, but today I want you to change the way you see! Start to see with My eyes and when you do that, your whole perspective will change!"

So I have an important question for you.

How do you see yourself today?

Most Christians would say that they do see themselves through God's eyes some of the time, but they also acknowledge that often they are dominated by their circumstances, since these speak so loudly.

The goal is to progress from seeing through God's eyes "some of the time" to "all of the time."

I was sharing this principle with a group of people recently and a young man waited afterwards until everyone else had left to speak to me personally. He was a very striking young man and looked incredibly fit. I discovered he was the regional director of a major national fitness phenomenon. He was well groomed and spoke articulately. He shared that he had a beautiful wife and family. Despite all this I could tell he was very distressed.

As he talked with his head down, he started to weep. He shared, "All my life my father and my mother as well as my brothers and sister told me that I was nothing but trash. Growing up, people treated me like trash and told me I was good for nothing. You asked us what we see when we look at ourselves. I just see trash."

This wonderful young man had been subject to the negativity of others for so long that when he looked at himself, he saw nothing good – only rubbish!

But God doesn't see him or you that way! He sees you as perfect in every way!

When God looks at you He sees you through the finished work of the cross!

He sees you complete! Nothing lacking or missing!

When you tell God about things that you think are lacking and missing in your life, He doesn't know what you are talking about.

He doesn't see you that way at all! He sees you as absolutely unique! There is only one of you. God sees you as so perfect He broke the mold after creating you. In this light, if you are someone who is constantly spending your time and money to change the way you look, my question would be, "Why?"

May the eyes of your heart be enlightened

When we were at Bible college we were taught that the way to improve our identity in Christ was to look into a mirror and declare who we were in Him every day. The idea was that this would help us to become sure of our identity. It was a hard thing to do, and with little result. In truth, it didn't bring about any real change inside me because I didn't see myself with God's eyes.

I have since discovered that the best way to discover your true identity is to have an intimacy encounter with the Father heart of God. I'll share my personal experience and insights in an upcoming chapter. Once you know that you are God's beloved son or daughter, your identity takes on its true character.

Paul prayed for us in Ephesians 1:17–18,

> I keep asking that the God of our Lord Jesus Christ, the glorious Father, may give you the Spirit of wisdom and revelation, so that you may know him better. I pray that the eyes of your heart may be enlightened...

Why did Paul pray that way? For you to SEE!

To *SEE* what?

Continuing in Ephesians 1:18–19,

> In order that you may know the hope to which he has called you, the riches of his glorious inheritance in his holy people, and his incomparably great power for us who believe.

Paul wants us to change the way we see so we will experience... (Ephesians 1:19–21)

> That power is the same as the mighty strength he exerted when he raised Christ from the dead and seated him at his right hand in the heavenly realms, far above all rule and authority, power and dominion, and every name that is invoked, not only in the present age but also in the one to come.

This is a whole new level of heavenly seeing!

So many Christians are taught that when they invite Jesus into their hearts He lives there, but that is not quite true. The Spirit of God, the Holy Spirit, is the One the Father sends to dwell in us. He is our helper! His Kingdom comes and lives inside us.

Jesus the Christ, according to Ephesians 1, sits on the right hand of the Father, and every circumstance that you will ever walk through and everything that you will ever be subject to is under His feet. Do you believe that?

Wait – it gets even better. Ephesians 2:6–7 says,

> And God raised us up with Christ and seated us with him in the heavenly realms in Christ Jesus, in order that in the coming ages he might show the incomparable riches of his grace, expressed in his kindness to us in Christ Jesus.

If you begin to see yourself sitting with Jesus with all your circumstances under your feet, your life perspective will change dramatically. Instead of looking up at your circumstances from the bottom of the mountain, look down on them with a heavenly perspective. They will look so much smaller than they previously appeared!

But there is another step you can take to make your seeing transformation complete. As you are seated with Him in your sonship, turn your head and look into the eyes of the Father God. When you gaze upon His majesty and look into

His eyes, everything changes! From there you can't help but look at life differently.

Why? It is because you have your Father's eyes. And once that happens you will have a whole new level of heavenly seeing.

This transformation in our seeing was done for us on the cross, too.

When Jesus was hanging on the cross, He said, "It is finished." At that moment He took the sins of all humankind once and for all eternity.

2 Corinthians 5:21 tells us that,

> God made him who had no sin to be sin for us, so that in him we might become the righteousness of God.

Not only is our sin finished – our breakthrough is finished! There is a victory over all your circumstances through the cross of Christ.

When you believe that about yourself it changes the way you see!

Be careful of others projecting their wrong seeing onto you.

In 1989 we moved with our five small children to the United States so I could study at Fuller Theological Seminary in Pasadena. Since most American families include only two children or less, people were often incredulous when they saw us with our little brood in public. Complete strangers would walk up to us in the supermarket and ask with a horrified look, "Are they all yours?"

I got so tired of this happening that one day I decided to give a cheeky answer to see what would happen. I responded, "This is just half of them, the other half are at home." The shock on their faces was priceless until I said, "I'm only joking."

What were they doing? They were projecting their wrong seeing onto me.

They projected their perspective of what was the politically correct number for a family onto everyone else, making a judgment on those who didn't live the way they saw life. I learned a valuable lesson through that experience. We all see life differently.

This is an important lesson you must learn so you are careful not to project your seeing onto others. It is also one of the best ways to learn to be patient with the spiritual growth of others. Everyone is at a different place in their growth journey.

The Word is our absolute

However, there is one override to this principle. You must always see God's Word as the absolute basis or anchor of your values and outlook in life. Otherwise you will never get God's perspective.

During the time we lived in the United States we had very little income, since I was a full-time student. But we did not let that restrict our faith to see that God is good and that He is the God of the impossible.

My family and I returned to Australia in 1993. After being back in Australia for only 12 months we were able to miraculously buy land on a golf course and build our family home there. It was and still is a remarkable testimony of the blessing of God when you live God's way.

When the owner of the construction company that was building our home discovered we had four daughters, he told us we needed a large mirror in our bathroom. "As they grow into teenagers, they will all want to use the mirror at the same time," he alerted. We agreed and followed his advice.

My wife is a very wise and wonderful mother. She knew that teenage girls are very susceptible to image problems and spending too much time in front of a mirror. So she put up a little sign on the mirror that said, *"For every minute of mirror time, you need to spend a minute in God's Word."*

Why?

My wife knew that she had to shape which perspective our daughter's eyes were SEEING. And the best mirror to do that is the mirror of God's Word. It is the reflection that comes from what God says about you.

How does God see you?

In God's eyes, you are absolutely amazing. He is full of awe when He looks at you.

When I share this statement in churches around the world, I sense people reacting to what I just said. They have been so conditioned by what the world says is beautiful or perfect that they believe just the opposite of what God says about their looks and their lives.

The truth is, God doesn't make junk!

Everything He makes is amazing. Including you.

He SEES you as His son or daughter!

> Say it with me,
>
> "GOD SEES ME AS HIS SON/HIS DAUGHTER!"

He sees you as royalty!

He sees you as a king and priest!

He sees you as holy!

He sees you as righteous, and the righteous are as bold as lions.

He sees you as a man of faith/woman of faith.

He sees you in His fullness.

He sees you complete in your destiny, not lacking in any way.

He sees you full of His power.

He sees you as perfect in every way with nothing needing to be changed.

Do you see yourself this way? If not, you need to!

That is your challenge: start seeing yourself the way God sees you.

Then you will start acting the way you see yourself!

WE WILL START ACTING ACCORDING TO THE WAY WE SEE OURSELVES

When a child begins school, their parents understand that at that age children grow quickly, so wise parents buy uniforms that are too big for their child. They know that by mid-year their child will have grown into the uniform.

Sometimes stepping into your future destiny may seem like this. Perhaps initially it doesn't look like anything you have imagined or seen. When you do step into it, by faith it feels too big for you at first. But if you start to see your future the way God sees it, it will cause a shift in your seeing and your thinking, and things will be released so that before you know it you will have grown into it.

SEE yourself as already restored!

SEE that the kingdom of God is already inside you!

SEE that you have stepped into this new season for your life, health, family, finances and your future! Then you will start acting the way you see yourself!

Transformation takes place

Transformation takes place when you SEE the way God sees you, SAY only what He commands you to say, and DO what HE says for you to do!

I hear the Lord say...

"You will be a fine-tuned instrument of faith!"

See yourself that way and say, "I am a fine-tuned instrument of faith."

"You will be a sharp piercing sword!"

See yourself as a powerful spiritual weapon of transformation that can even pierce discouragement, depression, deception, lack, and all types of evil.

"You are a potent force of love!"

See yourself overflowing with His love to everyone you meet today.

"You are full of faith and power!"

See yourself this way and faith and power will be your daily reality. It is a Seeing Transformation indeed.

Next stage

When you SEE with God's eyes, transformation takes place in you first.

Then the next stage of transformation happens. You transform the atmosphere around you wherever you go, including the darkest ungodly places. If you see yourself as an agent of transformation, you will take light into the darkest places.

You are a carrier of God's glory. His presence goes with you wherever you go!

> IF YOU SEE YOURSELF AS AN AGENT OF TRANSFORMATION YOU WILL TAKE LIGHT INTO THE DARKEST PLACES.

Paul says in 2 Corinthians 4:7–10,

> But we have this treasure in jars of clay to show that this all-surpassing power is from God and not from us. We are hard pressed on every side, but not crushed; perplexed, but not in despair; persecuted, but not abandoned; struck down, but not destroyed. We always carry around in our body the death of Jesus, so that the life of Jesus may also be revealed in our body.

I have three questions for you.

Close your eyes and think. Be as honest as you can with yourself.

First Question – How do I see myself today?

(Be really honest. It's not about the way you'd like to see yourself; rather, how do you truthfully see yourself?)

Take some time, and write it down here.

_____
_____
_____
_____
_____
_____

Second Question – How does God see me?

(Answer according to what God's Word says about you in context to what has been written in this chapter.)

Write it down here.

_____
_____
_____
_____
_____
_____

Third Question – Is there any difference between your answers to the first and second question?

_____
_____
_____
_____

If your seeing has truly been transformed, your answer should be, *"No Difference."*

From now on, choose to SEE and SAY only what He sees and says about you!

WHAT YOU SEE AND SAY IS WHAT YOU WILL BECOME

Then your seeing and your saying will become a reality…

See yourself whole, and you will become fully restored!

See yourself blessed, and you will become blessed!

See yourself healthy, and you will become full of health!

See yourself full of authority and power, and you will become full of God's authority and power!

See yourself full of faith and victory, and you will become just that!

See yourself fulfilling God's destiny for your life, and you will!

You keep going … SAY IT … Keep saying it…

The Seeing Transformation

What do you see?

_____
_____
_____
_____

Then you will BECOME what you SEE and SAY.

This is the key to living in remarkable miracles and spectacular victories.

This is the key to living free from discouragement.

This is the key to living a life of transformation.

Let's pray this into being right now!

> ### PRAY
>
> "Father, open my eyes to what You are seeing.
>
> Show me how I see You.
>
> Show me how I see the circumstances and obstacles in my life.
>
> Show me how I see myself.
>
> I make a decision to choose to SEE the way YOU SEE me, my circumstances and You.
>
> I choose to step out of the old way of Seeing into YOUR way of Seeing, Father.
>
> Right here. Right now!
>
> In Jesus' Name, Amen."

DECREE

Now let me make the following decree over you:

"I decree over you –

You have stepped into a seeing transformation.

You now see with God's eyes.

You see how He sees you and your life.

I decree your seeing and your saying will become a reality."

This is your Seeing Transformation.

CHAPTER 4

Unlocking Your Seeing to Live in the Miraculous

The next level of this Seeing Transformation is the realm of "remarkable miracles." The term *miracle* is used a lot these days.

So, what is a miracle?

A miracle is the supernatural intervention by the Spirit of God into the ordinary course of nature and life. God is the source of all miracles; however, some of His miracles actually happen through His sons and daughters – us!

My wife Cheryl and I have experienced remarkable miracles and blessings in the last few months – dramatic unexplained improvement of health in less than twenty four hours; supernatural cancellation of a large insurance debt; a number of unexpected windfalls, including long-term unpaid wages being paid at the same hour that we saw and decreed; new vehicles supplied; and our justice project for orphans in Kenya take off after years of it being stalled. Of course the greatest miracle of all is when someone who has not experienced the amazing grace and love of Jesus Christ receives Him as their Lord and Savior. The Bible says at that moment you move from eternal death to eternal life. If you have not yet received the miracle of eternity, it can become yours today.

(If you would like to know how to experience this incredible miracle, see Endnotes at the end of this book.)[1]

Astounding events such as these keep happening on a daily basis.

Extraordinary miracles

Many people believe that you have to be someone special, chosen by God – to SEE extraordinary miracles. But that is not the truth. The Bible is full of examples of God using ordinary people willing to obey Him to do miraculous things. All it takes is a desire to see God move in the lives of those around us. Over and over again we have seen this happen as we travel in Australia and around the world.

One of our daughters shared with us the following most remarkable miracle. A friend of hers had recently given birth to a baby boy. The doctors were concerned because he was

CHAPTER 4: UNLOCKING YOUR SEEING ... MIRACULOUS

> YOU DO NOT HAVE TO BE SOMEONE SPECIAL, CHOSEN BY GOD, TO SEE EXTRAORDINARY MIRACLES. GOD USES ORDINARY PEOPLE WILLING TO OBEY HIM TO DO MIRACULOUS THINGS.

not responding to the normal cognitive tests. They told the parents to take the baby to a specialist when he was three months old. They agreed, but they also prayed. They had learned not to look at their circumstances but at the promises God had given them. They started to decree that their baby boy was perfect in every way and nothing was missing or lacking. Three months later when they took him to be tested, the baby failed all the tests. The doctor told them he was profoundly deaf and was also blind. The parents asked the doctor to test the baby again. Reluctantly the doctor agreed. The test began and there was still no response from the baby. Then something dramatic happened. The baby's eyes followed the doctor's hand as he moved it past the baby's face. This had not happened before. Again and again the baby's eyes followed the doctor's movements. He also started to turn his head to noises in the room. The baby who moments before had been blind and deaf could now see and hear! It was an extraordinary miracle. The doctor was flabbergasted. He could not explain what had just happened. All he could do was to join in with the parents who were crying tears of joy. Our daughter's friends' SEEING moved their baby from a lifetime of hardship without sight and sound to a normal, healthy, happy person.

We have seen God miraculously break into the lives of supermarket employees, hotel receptionists, car rental clerks and people in coffee shops. God moves in the hearts of those who are hungry and will listen. But it's not just the good news of God's love that we must share – we must also be willing to step into the seeing realm of miracles. I call them remarkable miracles because each one is uniquely miraculous.

Encounters with Jesus

Peter encountered this realm of remarkable miracles in Luke 5. After a long night of hard work, Simon and his fellow fishermen had not caught anything. They were washing their nets when Jesus came along. The crowd was so large that Jesus climbed into Simon Peter's boat and began to teach the crowd from there.

When He had finished speaking, He told Peter to push his boat back into deep water and let down his nets again. Peter obeyed, even though he and his friends were exhausted. What happened next was remarkable.

Luke 5:6–9 says,

> When they had done so, they caught such a large number of fish that their nets began to break. So they signaled their partners in the other boat to come and help them, and they came and filled both boats so full that they began to sink.

When Simon Peter saw this, he fell at Jesus' knees and said, "Go away from me, Lord; I am a sinful man!" For he and all his companions were astonished at the catch of fish they had taken.

At that moment Peter saw who Jesus truly was – the Son of God! It convicted him of his sin as it showed him how distant he actually was from God. Fear is a natural response of a person who is not close to God. A consequence of your sin is that it causes you to run away from God and to reject Him even more. But the answer is just the reverse. When you begin to see God as He truly is, this is the time when you need to run to Him!

They were not just astonished at the huge number of fish in their nets, they SAW who Jesus truly was and it astonished them!

After that, all heaven broke loose (Luke 5:12–25). People were healed from leprosy. News about Jesus began to spread all over, and the crowds of people grew larger and larger. Later in the chapter we read that people couldn't get close enough for Jesus to heal them. The friends of a paralyzed man climbed up on the roof and broke a hole in it. Then they lowered the man down on a mat so Jesus could heal him. Jesus told the paralyzed man to get up, take up his mat and go home. He did just that. He went home praising God for his miracle.

The response of the people indicates the impact of the miracles that had taken place.

Luke 5:26 says,

> Everyone was amazed and gave praise to God. They were filled with awe and said, "We have seen remarkable things today."

When God manifests who He truly is and His people begin to SEE Him this way, then the realm of miracles becomes a normal experience.

A SEASON OF AWE

We have stepped into a season of awe – awesome miracles! It is possible to be filled with awe every day, not just occasionally. Cheryl and I have chosen to live in this realm of remarkable miracles in this season of awe. We are currently seeing miracles more and more each week, as we SEE this as normal lifestyle.

This new realm will enable you to experience remarkable miracles from Him and remarkable things for Him every day!

God wants you to step into this realm. It is the realm of the "greater things" that Jesus spoke about in John 14:12:

> "Very truly I tell you, whoever believes in me will do the works I have been doing, and they will do even greater things than these."

A friend of mine, a young, emerging Australian apostle, just came back after holding healing evangelistic crusades in Papua, New Guinea. Each night thousands of people accepted Jesus Christ as their Lord and Savior, and hundreds were physically healed. People with damaged limbs were completely healed, deaf people were able to hear again, and even a few blind people's eyes were opened and they saw! But one day my friend and his team were asked to go to the home of a young man who had just been killed in a car accident. They prayed for him for hours but he was not raised from the dead. Even though they had seen so many other miracles, and thousands come to Christ, they were not satisfied. When my friend and his team returned home, they fasted for 21 days because they were determined to see a greater manifestation of the realm of the "greater things."

When I heard his story, it made me hungry for the "greater things," too. And I am sure you also feel that way now.

> Decree it now:
> "IT'S TIME FOR THE 'GREATER THINGS' IN MY LIFE RIGHT HERE, RIGHT NOW!"

How? We need to see what God sees!

Jeremiah's response

In Jeremiah's case this should have been straightforward. God's call on Jeremiah's life is recorded in Jeremiah 1:4–5,

> The word of the Lord came to me, saying,
> "Before I formed you in the womb I knew you,

> Before you were born I set you apart;
> I appointed you as a prophet to the nations."

God's call upon Jeremiah was very powerful, but Jeremiah could not see it! In fact, Jeremiah's initial response in verse 6 was,

> "Alas, Sovereign Lord ... I do not know how to speak; I am too young."

Why?

Jeremiah's SEEING needed to be transformed. What and how much you experience in the remarkable is directly affected by your capacity to SEE. The problem is, most of us live according to what we naturally see, NOT what God supernaturally sees!

Jeremiah could only see with His limited, natural, circumstance-controlled eyes. In reality he had an orphan heart, which we speak of in more detail in a later chapter. He was NOT seeing how God saw him!

We Are children of the King of Kings

God sees you as his son or daughter. You are a child of the King of Kings – you are royalty!

Some friends received this revelation recently. It so powerfully changed the way they saw themselves that everywhere they went people treated them as royalty. After working very hard in their own business for over thirty years without a decent vacation, they decided to book a holiday for a two-week

CHAPTER 4: UNLOCKING YOUR SEEING ... MIRACULOUS

South Pacific cruise. They used their points on their credit card to pay for the cruise months in advance, and a specific room was reserved in their name. A few weeks before their departure date, they called to confirm their booking, only to find that the cruise line had given their room to someone else who had paid cash. There were no other cabins left on that deck of the ship. In fact, the whole cruise was booked except for the best stateroom on the ship – the royal suite. However, they were told that they didn't have enough points to afford it. After getting off the phone, they prayed together. They reminded the Lord that they were indeed royalty, so the royal suite belonged to them. Then they called their credit card company and informed them what had happened. Since the cruise line had done the wrong thing, their credit card company challenged the company to fix it and asked for the royal suite. Reluctantly, the cruise line conceded the suite to my friends. As they boarded the ship, everyone else had to line up, but they were given privileged entry. Then, when they opened the door to the suite, they were amazed. It consisted of multiple rooms, including their own dining room and food buffet. Everything was luxurious. It was fit for a king and queen indeed.

They fell on their knees as they worshipped the Lord, laughing and crying at how the Lord sees them as royalty. Then there was a knock on the door. It was a crew member. He said, "Hi, my name is Jesus and I am your butler and assistant for the whole cruise." They were overwhelmed at how God moves in our lives once we start to see ourselves the way

He sees us. Later during the cruise they were able to pray with their new friend Jesus, who was from the Philippines, and introduced him to Jesus Christ as Lord and Savior.

Encounters that bring change

Your challenge is to start seeing yourself more and more the way God sees you. Otherwise, God's response to you today is the same as it was for Jeremiah in Jeremiah 1:7.

> *"Do not say,* 'I am too young.' You must go to everyone I send you to and say whatever I command you." *(emphasis added)*

He continues in verse 8,

> "Do not be afraid of them, *for I am with you and will rescue you,*" declares the Lord. *(emphasis added)*

And there's still more in verse 9,

> Then the Lord reached out his hand and touched my mouth and said to me, "I have put my words in your mouth."

You have to have a God encounter to change the way you speak. Then you will only speak His words about your circumstances.

Your words will affect the way you see!

Your words speak what is in your heart!

Chapter 4: Unlocking Your Seeing ... Miraculous

Let's continue with God's message to Jeremiah, verse 10,

> SEE, today I appoint you over nations and kingdoms to uproot and tear down, to destroy and overthrow, to build and to plant."

"Whoever says to this mountain…"

In Mark 11:23, Jesus teaches about faith in God. Notice He links your believing to your saying.

> "Whoever SAYS to this mountain, 'Be removed and be cast into the sea,' and does not doubt in his heart, but believes that those things he SAYS will be done, he will have whatever he SAYS." *(uppercase added)*

Before you say it, you have to SEE it with your transformed eyes of faith.

Think again about the young girl in Kenya in chapter one who was healed of blindness. She first had to see in faith and then she saw physically. Her seeing and her saying transformed her reality.

What do you say today about *your* life?

Are you speaking about your problems or your solutions?

Are speaking about your struggle or your victory?

Perhaps you need to turn and look into His eyes until you see the way He sees. Then say what you see, and your saying will affect your reality, too!

Seeing with God's eyes unlocks remarkable favor

Cheryl and I have experienced a whole new realm of seeing the miraculous since we had the supernatural encounter with Shawn Bolz in Pasadena. Shortly after returning home I woke up one morning at 3:05 a.m. and heard the Lord say, "Read Psalm 30:5."

Most Christians will be familiar with the second part of this verse:

> Weeping may stay for the night, but rejoicing comes in the morning.

But the beginning of this verse says:

> For his anger lasts only a moment, but his FAVOR lasts a lifetime;

I heard the Lord say, "Tell them, 'Your season of weeping is over. Now it is time for a lifetime of favor.'"

It is time to step into a lifetime of favor. It is not just any favor. It is the remarkable favor of God. When you do, you will see the supernatural break into your natural circumstances, and miracles will begin to occur.

What do you see?

It was true for Jeremiah, it will be true for us! Let's continue with his story in Jeremiah 1:11.

> The word of the Lord came to me: "What do you see, Jeremiah?"

Something glorious had happened! Jeremiah changed the way he saw himself! It opened his spiritual eyes and he saw into the supernatural. What did he see in the supernatural?

"I see the branch of an almond tree,"

God's response was *"You have seen correctly!"* Then God says something very significant, not only for Jeremiah but for you, in verse 12.

"I am watching to SEE that my word is fulfilled."

When our seeing changes, it releases God's supernatural favor into our circumstances. The New King James (NKJV) translation of verse 12 says it this way,

"I am watching [overseeing] over my word to perform it."

This is good news for you today. When you begin to see with God's eyes, it opens up a whole new dimension of supernatural miracles.

An extraordinary financial miracle

Just recently one of my daughters had a car accident. Even though she was not hurt, she called us with some very upsetting news. She had overlooked paying her car insurance renewal and the insurance company was refusing her claim because her insurance had lapsed. There was over $10,000 damage to her car and nearly $7,000 to the other car. The accident was her fault so she was liable for this entire amount. She told us that she had appealed the insurance company's decision, offering to pay the overdue renewal amount. The appeal process would take five days. My wife and I were initially concerned because we were looking with natural eyes. I reasoned, what business would give you $17,000 if they didn't legally have to?

My daughter challenged our incorrect seeing. She asked us to come into agreement with her husband and her. We agreed and changed our seeing. Then we asked God to release His supernatural favor. A few days later she called, shouting praise into the phone. The insurance company had changed their mind and had honored the insurance claim. She had just experienced supernatural debt cancellation. It was an extraordinary miracle. What looked entirely impossible became possible because she saw with God's perspective.

Seeing with God's perspective opens up a whole new way of seeing, and God loves you to see this way. He then takes the responsibility to shift your circumstances. What you see in the supernatural He creates in the natural for you! His words will become flesh for you, too!

We act the way we see ourselves. When our seeing changes it releases God's remarkable miracles into our normal circumstances.

SEEING UNLOCKS YOU TO BE A REMARKABLE MIRACLE TO OTHERS

The last stage of stepping into the realm of seeing remarkable miracles is when we see others with God's eyes.

Chapter 4: Unlocking Your Seeing ... Miraculous

When you see with God's eyes, you see others with His love. Your whole mindset shifts from God and you to God and others. You are motivated to love in the most selfless way. This is what it means to be a true disciple of Christ.

Remarkable miracles start to happen for others when you begin to see them with God's eyes of love!

In Jeremiah 1:13, God asks Jeremiah again,

"What do you see?"

Jeremiah answers,

"I see a pot that is boiling," I answered. "It is tilting toward us from the north."

His seeing moved from himself onto others. In this case it had moved onto his nation Israel and he saw disaster was coming from the north. This moved Jeremiah that day from being merely a seer to becoming a transformer for a whole nation!

God is asking the same question today – *What do you see?*

> WHEN YOU SEE WITH GOD'S EYES, YOU SEE OTHERS WITH HIS LOVE. YOUR WHOLE MINDSET SHIFTS FROM GOD AND YOU TO GOD AND OTHERS.

When you start to truly see, then you will be able to do what He says. This is the key to living in the seeing realm of remarkable miracles.

Choose to only believe what He sees and you will unlock the miraculous and live in the miracles of God every day!

Make a decision to choose to SEE the way God sees YOU and step into the realm of remarkable miracles and spectacular victories.

PRAY

Lord Jesus, Open my eyes to the way I have been seeing.

I choose to change the way I SEE to your way of seeing.

Help me to change the way I SPEAK so I only SAY what you SEE!

Move my seeing from ME to OTHERS.

In Jesus' name, Amen.

CHAPTER 5

Wrong Seeing

Things don't always appear as they are!

As a young boy I desperately wanted to grow up to play rugby football for our national team. Representing Australia was every little school boy's dream. But there was a problem. I was too skinny and did not have the right build for a rugby player. But I could not see that! So I persevered for years even after multiple injuries, until one day I realized that I was a better long distance runner than a ball player. I'd had a wrong perception for all those years. When I changed the focus of my training, my sense of fulfillment and enjoyment went to a whole new level.

I could have been a top long distance runner but I couldn't see it when I was young, and my subsequent knee injuries prevented me from achieving what I was really good at. This is what wrong seeing does. It steals from your ability to see your life and future clearly.

Our seeing can be Affected by loss, trauma and grief

The story of Jesus' crucifixion is traumatic. I can't even begin to imagine what it was like for the disciples who were there that day. They witnessed the agonizing death of the Messiah whom they had all been waiting for, the One sent by God to deliver Israel. But Jesus was even more than that to them. He was their Lord, their Master, their Teacher, their everything! So to see Him mocked, tortured and crucified surely brought them extreme shock and grief. Their world had just been turned upside down and shattered.

Emotion, pain and grief do many things to people. One of the greatest things it does is change the way we see. The disciples had lost all hope. Their trauma and grief had clouded their minds and their perception. It even caused them to forget Jesus' teaching.

Mary and other women went to the tomb early Sunday morning. When she arrived there she found the stone rolled away and immediately assumed the worst.

Even though she could see two angels inside the empty tomb, John 20:14 says,

> At this, she turned around and saw Jesus standing there, but she did not realize that it was Jesus.

Chapter 5: Wrong Seeing

She saw Jesus standing there but she did not SEE Him! Verse 15 says,

> He asked her, "Woman, why are you crying? Who is it you are looking for?"

Often the things we are looking for in life are right in front of us! That is true on so many levels. Mary thought Jesus was the gardener, so she said to Him in verse 15,

> Sir, if you have carried him away, tell me where you have put him, and I will get him.

Mary assumed that because Jesus was no longer in His tomb, someone had taken Him – but that was not the case at all! In fact nothing could be further from the truth. He had risen from the dead just as He had told them.

Mary's seeing was colored by loss, trauma, and grief. When you make assumptions based on pain, fears or an orphan heart, you see wrongly. Not only is your perception wrong, but also your ability to see supernaturally is greatly inhibited – to the degree that it is nearly impossible to see

> **WHEN YOU MAKE ASSUMPTIONS BASED ON PAIN, FEARS OR AN ORPHAN HEART, YOU SEE WRONGLY. NOT ONLY IS YOUR PERCEPTION WRONG, BUT ALSO YOUR ABILITY TO SEE SUPERNATURALLY IS GREATLY INHIBITED.**

supernaturally. Mary even thought the gardener had taken Him. This is what wrong perception does – it clouds your judgment and you see things the wrong way. It was only when Jesus spoke her name *Mary* that her eyes were opened.

> She turned toward him and cried out in Aramaic, "Rabboni!" (which means "Teacher"). (v. 16)

My mother taught me growing up "not to judge a book by its cover." In other words, do not judge others by how they look on the outside. I have to admit I haven't always taken my mother's advice. Why? My seeing was not with the eyes of God. So some of my greatest joys as a Christian leader have been discovering the depth of love and wisdom in some least-likely looking people.

Correcting Our seeing

So how do we learn to have right seeing?

1. Begin with a humble heart

When we are subject to others' wrong perceptions, we are often tempted to defend ourselves or try to clarify their perception. But that is the Lord's job, not ours. My spiritual father, Ché Ahn, teaches that the key is not to react to others' wrong perception of you. This is important for a number of reasons. Primarily, when we defend ourselves we typically react out of our orphan heart. On the other hand, when you absorb criticism, it causes you to respond in humility and love. The more you respond in humility and love, the clearer your spirit man is able to hear God's voice and see what He is doing.

I have also learned that what appears on the surface to be true often isn't – especially when it appears someone is either being negative or critical of you. I have learned from Patricia King to keep humble and always respond in love. She speaks about always keeping low and beginning small.

Peter and James, as well as the Proverbs, teach us,

"God opposes the proud, but gives grace to the humble." (Proverbs 3:34; 1 Peter 5:5 and James 4:6)

Humility positions your heart so you are able to see and hear clearly. Pride does exactly the opposite.

2. Encounter the Father Heart of God

Everyone of us needs to have an intimate encounter with the Father heart of God. As Bill Johnson teaches, only then will we truly know who we are in Christ and walk in His authority. When I first experienced God as my Father, the realm of the supernatural exploded.

In 2008 during a visit to Iris ministries in Mozambique, I had an amazing experience that changed my life dramatically. During the Sunday morning church service, Heidi Baker invited all visitors to come forward and allow the orphaned children to pray for them individually. While the congregation worshipped for a lengthy time – as is usual in Heidi Baker's meetings – two little children prayed for me.

One was seven years old and the other was ten years old. Usually small children don't pray very long, but this was very different. After their first ten minutes of prayer, my thoughts were that it had been a long time since anyone had prayed for me for that length of time. For fifteen minutes they had been praying that I experience God's Father heart when I realized that the children praying for me were not orphans, since they had been adopted by Mama Heidi. In fact, I was the orphan. After another ten minutes of prayer, something remarkable happened. I looked up to the top of the tent, and in the spirit I saw a scroll floating down to me. I asked the Lord, "What is that, Father?" He replied, *"Those are your adoption papers. Welcome home, son."*

So many things changed in my life that day. After I returned home, members of my congregation came up to me saying, "You have changed. There is something different about you." They were right. I *had* changed. For the first time in my life I knew I was truly loved and accepted by my Father in heaven. My prayer life changed. The way I saw others changed. I even began to look differently at those behaving badly. I realized that an orphan spirit in their heart caused them to act and react the way they did. Typically their poor attitude towards me was because they had been treated badly earlier in their lives by father figures who should have known better, but didn't. Why? Because they too were spiritual orphans and not true fathers.

Another unexpected benefit of experiencing the Father heart of God was that the realm of the supernatural became commonplace in my life. In my book, *Encountering the Supernatural*, I explain a lot more about this.

To be truly led by the spirit of God, it is vital that we step into our true identity as sons and daughters of Father God.

Romans 8:14 (NASB) says,

> For all who are being led by the Spirit of God, these are sons of God."

Paul goes on to say that we receive a *spirit of adoption*, which results in us becoming sons and daughters of God.

We will speak some more about this later in the next chapter, "Unlocking the Things that Stop your Seeing."

I encourage you to stop right now and ask Father God to reveal more of His Father heart to you. Be bold enough to ask Him to show you what things in your life reflect an orphan heart. And then allow His Father's love to work in you, changing you, healing you, setting you free.

Something wonderful will begin to happen. You will start to see clearly. And wrong seeing will occur less frequently in your life.

CHAPTER 6

Unlocking the Things that Stop Your Seeing

TRUE IDENTITY CAUSES US TO SEE

Identity is very important. Unfortunately, most people equate identity with physical appearance. Media bombards you constantly, telling you that you need to purchase their products, commit to certain activities or even go through extreme procedures in order to be attractive, popular or successful. It makes me smile when I go to African nations and notice young women applying lotions on their skin to look whiter. Then when I return home to Australia I see women going to tanning salons, sun-baking or even using spray tans to make their skin look browner.

Advertising for diet supplements and gymnasiums promise you a whole new body. Now we have the tattoo craze that involves people often spending thousands of dollars to permanently mark their bodies. Then there are those who identify with the hipster trend in the United States – they are constantly changing clothing, hairstyle, music artists, and restaurants to reinforce their cool identity.

There will always be someone trying to convince you that you need to change something else to be confident about who you are and what you look like. But nothing could be further from what makes up your real identity.

God the Father is the one who made you, so what He says is all that really matters. When you begin to hear what He really thinks about you, you will change the way you see yourself.

On the other hand, the lack of God-inspired identity steals your intimacy and authority in God.

Jesus' identity was one of the targets of Satan's attacks when He went in the wilderness to fast and pray for 40 nights. But He refused to allow His identity to be challenged. Neither should you allow your identity to be undermined.

Hebrews 4:15 says it this way,

> For we do not have a high priest who is unable to empathize with our weaknesses, but we have one who has been tempted in every way, just as we are – yet he did not sin.

Satan also challenged Jesus' intimacy with the Father and His authority. Because Jesus overcame these temptations, Jesus grew in His power and authority. So will you.

YOUR TRUE IDENTITY COMES FROM INTIMACY WITH GOD THE FATHER.

As stated previously, your identity begins to become unlocked when you have an intimacy encounter with God. We have already discussed this briefly, but let's go deeper.

> UNTIL YOU HAVE AN ENCOUNTER WITH THE SPIRIT OF ADOPTION FROM THE FATHER, YOU WILL CONTINUE TO SEE YOURSELF AND LIVE AS AN ORPHAN.

Many people have problems relating to God as a loving heavenly Father because of lack of love from father figures when they were younger. But it actually goes deeper than this. The truth is that until you have an encounter with the spirit of adoption from the Father, you will continue to see yourself and live as an orphan.

Romans 8:14–16 says,

> For those who are led by the Spirit of God are the children of God. The Spirit you received does not make you slaves,

so that you live in fear again; rather, the Spirit you received brought about your adoption to sonship. And by him we cry, *"Abba Father."* The Spirit himself testifies with our spirit that we are God's children.

At the Australian Apostolic Restore Community (A.A.R.C.)[1] we lead Father's Heart Encounters throughout Australia and other nations. We teach people how to have an "intimacy encounter" with the Father heart of God, then we help them experience such an encounter. These have helped many people to experience the spirit of adoption and be released from an orphan heart.

If they have encountered God's Father heart before, then our goal is to lead them into a deeper encounter with Abba Father God. The testimonies are amazing. We have so many people who want to share their encounter that we always run out of time.

Another key to knowing your true identity is to recognize the existence of shame, fear and control in your life

During the the Father's Heart Encounters we also share a powerful teaching on the SHAME, FEAR, CONTROL Stronghold from Restoring the Foundations Ministry.[1]

As a result, attendees now have some excellent tools that help them to walk out of an orphan heart and experience more of the spirit of adoption for their lives on an ongoing basis. It is wonderful to hear from people for weeks and months afterwards of how much their lives have changed.

The "Shame, Fear, Control" stronghold is based on Genesis 3:10, where Adam said:

"I was afraid because I was naked; so I hid."

When Adam said he was naked, he was displaying shame. Shame lies to you about who you are and how you see yourself. Shame caused Adam to say, *"I believe that I am flawed."* It changed the way Adam SAW himself – he moved from God's way of seeing *"perfect in every way"* to seeing himself as "naked." He was no longer clothed with God's way of seeing.

The fear stronghold holds us back from seeing who we truly are. Adam said, *"I was afraid."*

What made him afraid? Fear entered when he started using worldly seeing. Once he sinned, he became fearful that people would find out what he really was like and would not like him, and even reject him. Fear stops us from seeing ourselves God's way.

Adam expressed control when he said, *"so I hid."* When you try to control your life, others, and your circumstances, you are trying to protect yourself from more pain. The trouble with control is that in the process you pretend to be someone who you are not.

So shame, fear and control actually hides your true identity. The good news is that God wants to set you free to be your true self. The more you reduce fear and shame and control in your life, the more freedom you have to step into a true identity.

Isaiah 61:7 (NKJV) says it like this,

> Instead of your shame *you shall have* DOUBLE *HONOR*, and *instead* of confusion they shall rejoice in their portion. Therefore in their land they shall possess double; everlasting joy shall be theirs.

Disabling fear

As we mentioned above, fear is one of the principal hindrances to seeing with God's eyes. You have heard the expression, "blinded by fear." That is exactly how fear works. It deceives, making you look or see in a way that is not true.

Fear can be defined by the acronym F.E.A.R.

F – False

E – Evidence

A – Appearing

R – Real

Fear is the exact opposite to the truth. The heart of fear is to undermine who you really are. It can steal your voice, your authority, and your identity. You need to resist all fear! The best way to do this is to see things as they truly are. Fear is like a cataract over your eyes that stops you from seeing clearly.

It is always important to find out the truth about the situation you are potentially facing. Jesus said, "You will know the truth, and the truth will set you free" (John 8:32).

Everytime a lie comes at you, find out what God's Word says and choose to only believe the truth about that circumstance. Meditate on that truth and then decree it until peace fills your heart and fear leaves your mind and emotions.

Two different responses

Who you become and the fulfillment of your purpose does not depend on what happens to you in life, but on how you respond when those life events happen.

In Luke, chapter 1, the angel Gabriel appears to two different people. Both were initially afraid of what they saw. Then only one could truly see what the angel was saying.

Gripped by fear – Zachariah

In Luke 1:11, the angel of the Lord appeared to Zachariah. He was in the temple ministering to God. Verse 12 says,

> When Zachariah saw him, he was startled and was gripped with fear.

The angel then spoke to him reassuringly, "Do not be afraid, Zechariah; your prayer has been heard" (v. 13). But even though Zachariah heard what the angel Gabriel said, he could not "SEE" it:

"How can I be sure of this? I am an old man and my wife is well along in years" (v. 18). Zachariah had an orphan heart. Instead of being able to believe what the angel was saying was true, all he could do was be afraid. The stronghold of fear stopped his true identity from being displayed. But there were even greater consequences. His fear shut his mouth. It stopped his true identity as a prophet of God from speaking out, according to verse 20:

> "And now you will be silent and not be able to speak until the day this happens, because you did not believe my words, which will come true at their appointed time."

Zachariah's destiny as a seer of God was limited because of his fear. Don't let fear blind your seeing and prevent you from fulfilling your God-destiny.

Keys to getting rid of blinding fear

Refuse to allow fear in your seeing any more. Let's briefly review the following keys that will remove blinding fear and help us see with God's eyes.

1. Experience the true love of God

1 John 4:18 says,

> There is no fear in love. But perfect love drives out fear, because fear has to do with punishment. The one who fears is not made perfect in love.

2. Look only at God's promise to you – not at your circumstances.

Your health prognosis, bank balance, debts, lack, and any other bad reports will only increase stress if you keep looking at them.

What does God say about this situation? Biblical decrees and meditating on what God sees and says about you will destroy all fear. Cheryl and I have found that these are the best antidotes to fear, and frequently use Patricia King's book, *Decree*.[2]

UNLOCKING FAITH-SEEING – MARY'S STORY

Faith and trust in God will unlock you to see powerfully.

You have a choice every day when you are confronted with your circumstances. Are you going to see through the eyes of "facts," or are you going to see through the eyes of faith?

The second person that the angel Gabriel appeared to in Luke chapter 1 responded in a totally different way. She was a young girl named Mary.

Even though Mary was also initially afraid when Gabriel appeared to her and told her that she was to become the mother of the Savior of the world, she did not refuse to believe; SHE SAW! Luke 1:38 says,

"I am the Lord's servant," Mary answered, "May your word to me be fulfilled." Then the angel left her.

Mary was able to give the right answer. She went from being "greatly troubled" to saying, "yes."

As a result, she saw the supernatural impact on her life and the rest is history!

WHAT she SAW changed her present, future and eternity. She SAW to the extent that the supernatural, through the Holy Spirit, physically impregnated her womb. She supernaturally got pregnant!

But she saw more than that. She also saw generationally!

How can I be sure of this? Just read her song of praise in Luke 1:46–49. Through the ages it has been known simply as "Mary's song," but we could also call it "Mary's supernatural seeing song."

> "My soul glorifies the Lord and my spirit rejoices in God my Savior, for he has been mindful of the humble state of his servant. From now on all generations will call me blessed, for the Mighty One has done great things for me – holy is his name."

Did you hear what she said? Or I should say, did you see what she saw? "From now on ALL generations will call me blessed."

But Mary was not done yet. Verse 50 says,

> MARY SAW GENERATIONS FOR HUNDREDS AND THOUSANDS OF YEARS TO COME RECEIVING THE SAVIOR OF THE WORLD INTO THEIR LIVES.

"His mercy extends to those who fear him, from generation to generation. He has performed mighty deeds with his arm."

Mary SAW it!

She saw generations for hundreds and thousands of years to come (including you) receiving the Savior of the world into their lives and being saved from the consequences of their sin and their eternal separation from God.

This is confirmed by verse 54,

> "He has helped his servant Israel, remembering to be merciful to Abraham and his descendants forever, just as he promised our ancestors."

In fact, she was more of a seer than Zachariah! Mary the young girl saw because she did not remain in the fear she first felt when the angel Gabriel appeared to her.

Instead she saw with the eyes of faith, and faith unlocked her destiny that day. This same faith unlocks your destiny to be fulfilled, too!

Good news

The good news is that it is never too late to start seeing with the eyes of faith!

Zechariah also received an opportunity to see with faith eyes. Even though he didn't respond well at the beginning, he finished well. He had plenty of time to change the way he saw when his tongue was silenced!

Luke 1:63–64 says,

> He asked for a writing tablet, and to everyone's astonishment he wrote, "His name is John." Immediately his mouth was opened and his tongue set free, and he began to speak, praising God.

But it doesn't stop there. Verse 67 says,

> Zachariah was filled with the Holy Spirit and prophesied.

Now he SAW and he SPOKE what he SAW.

Your seeing will unlock your saying

Your saying will always follow what you are seeing. In other words, your seeing and your words go together. You must speak what you see and see what you speak. And there is power in both. But there is even more power when they work together. This is another important reason your decrees are so important.

When Cheryl and I together first started to make decrees every day, the results were immediate and remarkable. We believed that God had prompted us to get out of debt. So we took a photo of our car and our house and placed it on our notice board in our house of prayer. When we started to decree together every day using Scriptures for God's Favor and Provision, all heaven broke loose. Within one week we received a phone call from a friend asking how he could help with the expenses for the transition in our ministry. I informed him of our basic ministry expenses such as our phone and website. But then he asked if there was anything else. I hesitated but he prompted me again, so I eventually told him about our monthly car lease. He paused, then told me he would pray and get back to me. A few days later he called to say God had told him to buy us a car.

Let me tell you that sort of thing had not happened to us before. But now, we see debt cancellation, unexpected inheritance, and incredible provision on a regular basis. All since we have changed the way we see and we say!

MIRACLES WILL HAPPEN

Make sure that nothing stops you from seeing the way God wants you to see! Once you change your seeing, it will unlock your saying. Then miracles will flow in your life, too!

In Mark 11:23 Jesus says,

> "Truly I tell you, if anyone SAYS to this mountain, 'Go, throw yourself into the sea,' and does not doubt in their heart but believes that what they SAY will happen, it will be done for them."

What an amazing promise! But you have to *see* it in faith before you can *say* it in faith! And then, don't just see it or say it once or occasionally. You need to learn to live in it every day. Make sure that nothing stops you from seeing the way God wants you to see. Initially, you might have to be constantly correcting your old way of seeing and saying. Keep doing it. Soon your seeing and your saying will change.

PRAYER:

"Lord Jesus, open my eyes. Show me if there are any fear or shame or control strongholds in my life that stop me from truly seeing my true identity in You. I decree that I open my heart to Your Father heart for me so I can step out of any fear in my heart today. I choose to respond in faith, knowing that my heavenly Father only has good things for me. I trust you completely. I step out of any wrong seeing and I choose to see the way you want me to see. I choose to SAY only what you SEE about me. I ask that you unlock faith-seeing in me, in Jesus' name. Amen."

CHAPTER 7

Seeing with Kingdom Eyes

PART 1

THE KINGDOM OF GOD HAS COME – CAN YOU SEE IT?

Recently there has been a lot of teaching on the kingdom of God, yet I still find that many Christians are unable to explain in their own words how the kingdom of God works – right now! Here on earth!

Why? They haven't truly SEEN the kingdom work in their lives.

How do you SEE the kingdom in such a way that you enable it to work through you today?

Jesus spent much of His time on earth teaching keys about the kingdom of God, but you have to SEE spiritually to understand them.

Mark 4:11 says,

> "The secret of the kingdom of God has been given to you."

If secrets have been given to you, then why don't you live them, or at least try to understand them?

The truth is, as Jesus said, most people are "ever seeing but never perceiving" (Mark 4:12). You need to see those secrets spiritually to truly understand what Jesus said!

Jesus either taught or demonstrated 12 times in the gospel of Mark how to SEE the kingdom of God work in your life.

Jesus teaches that the kingdom of heaven is like a seed inside of you.

The kingdom of God is ALWAYS increasing inside you!

Do you *see* it like that? If not, pray right now and ask the Father to change the way you see.

> "Father, I ask You to change the way I see the kingdom of God growing inside me NOW, in Jesus' name. Amen."

In Mark 4, Jesus said that the kingdom of God is like seed being planted in soil. It is alive and growing in us even if we cannot perceive it.

Chapter 7: Seeing with Kingdom Eyes - Part 1

> ONCE YOU LEARN TO FLOW WITH THE KINGDOM OF GOD GROWING INSIDE, YOU CAN EXPECT THE MIRACULOUS TO HAPPEN IN YOU AND THROUGH YOU.

Mark 4:26–29 says,

"This is what the kingdom of God is like. A man scatters seed on the ground. Night and day, whether he sleeps or gets up, the seed sprouts and grows, though he does not know how. All by itself the soil produces grain – first the stalk, then the head, then the full kernel in the head. As soon as the grain is ripe, he puts the sickle to it, because the harvester has come."

We might not understand how the kingdom of God works inside us, but know that it just does. It is always at work. Jesus also said in Luke 17:21 (NKJV),

"The kingdom of God is within you."

You simply have to accept that HIS kingdom is already inside you. The degree of growth of that kingdom seed is dependent on how fertile your mind, will and emotions are.

The sooner we understand that the kingdom of God is working in us and through us, the more effective the kingdom of God is in our lives. Once you learn to flow with the kingdom of God growing inside, you can expect the miraculous to happen in you and through you. This is how you can live a lifestyle of extraordinary miracles and spectacular victories.

Jesus teaches us that the kingdom of God grows, whether we SEE it or not.

Jesus takes it a step further. The kingdom of God is not like just any seed but a very special type of seed. He teaches us that the kingdom of God grows like a mustard seed inside of you.

Why a mustard seed?

Jesus answers that question in Mark 4:30–32,

> Again he said, "What shall we say the kingdom of God is like, or what parable shall we use to describe it? It is like a mustard seed, which is the smallest of all seeds on earth. Yet when planted, it grows and becomes the largest of all garden plants, with such big branches that the birds can perch in its shade."

Jesus is explaining how He can use anyone regardless of their past. Neither your background nor where you've come from matters. All that matters is your willingness to allow the kingdom of God to grow in you, so that then you can be used by God to spread that kingdom to every person that you meet. When the kingdom seed comes to life inside you, heaven begins to overflow in you and through you. One of the things that I love most about being a disciple of Jesus is that He does not discriminate between those He uses.

Your ability doesn't matter, either. What only matters is how willing you are for the seed of the kingdom of God to grow into a huge tree inside you. The size of the tree is not dependent on the size of the seed – rather, it depends on the size of the willing heart in which the seed is planted. My question to you today, is, *"Are you willing to allow God's kingdom seed to explode inside you from now on?"*

If you are, then stop for a moment now and surrender all of yourself to Jesus and invite Him to grow the kingdom of heaven inside of you!

Jesus demonstrates the kingdom to the disciples and to you so you can SEE it.

You can discover how the kingdom of heaven works in a number of ways. One of the best ways is SEEING it demonstrated to you.

Jesus was aware of this, so in Mark 4:35–41 we are told,

> That day when evening came, he said to his disciples "Let us go over to the other side." Leaving the crowd behind, they took him along, just as he was, in the boat. There were also other boats with him. A furious squall came up, and the waves broke over the boat, so that it was nearly swamped. Jesus was in the stern, sleeping on a cushion. The disciples woke him and said to him, "Teacher, don't you care if we drown?"

What Jesus did next was to demonstrate the kingdom of heaven in action on earth.

> He got up, rebuked the wind and said to the waves, "Quiet! Be still!" Then the wind died down and it was completely calm.

Do you think that you can do the same thing? The disciples didn't. That is why they were so full of fear.

> He said to his disciples, "Why are you so afraid? Do you still have no faith?" They were terrified and asked each other, "Who is this? Even the wind and the waves obey him!"

The disciples did not truly understand that the power of the kingdom of heaven was available to them, too! They thought that this type of kingdom living was only for Jesus the Messiah. The disciples could not SEE it. Why? Fear!

Fear stole their capacity to SEE. And fear will stop you from seeing, too!

My question to you today is, "Do you have fear that blinds your capacity to see in the spirit?"

Does this fear or intimidation paralyze you from stepping out boldly in faith?

If so, why don't you ask Him right now to set you free from all fear?

God's Word promises us in 2 Timothy 1:7 (NKJV),

> For God has not given us a spirit of fear, but of power and of love and of a sound mind."

The kingdom of heaven in you has power over demons.

When you truly understand that the kingdom of heaven is powerful and that power is inside you, nothing can oppose it – including evil and demons. So many Christians credit the devil and demons with much more power and influence than they actually have. Don't ever be afraid of demons.

You have to SEE God's kingdom inside you so that demons will be afraid of you. Then you will see demons in their true state:

They are defeated, and subject to YOU – "He gave them power and authority…"

Luke 9:1 says,

> When Jesus had called the Twelve together, he gave them power and authority to drive out all demons and to cure diseases.

In my book, *Encountering the Supernatural*, I teach how Jesus has given ALL believers authority to heal the sick and to cast out demons.[1]

Whenever I teach this in various settings, I ask the question, "Are there any believers here?" The majority of people raise their hands. However, I have realized that there are many "unbelieving believers" in the body of Christ today.

How can I say that? Well, most Christians don't believe Luke 9:1, or they would speak and act like they have power and authority over demons and disease. In fact, a lot of Christians are actually scared of the devil and demons.

How can I be so sure? Because they're always telling us how much the devil is oppressing them and giving them a hard time. The truth is the exact opposite.

In Mark 5, Jesus goes across the lake to the region of the Gerasenes. When Jesus gets out of the boat, a naked man who was possessed by many demons confronts him.

Was Jesus afraid? No! In fact just the opposite is true. The demons were afraid of Jesus!

Mark 5:6–8 says,

> When he saw Jesus from a distance, he ran and fell on his knees in front of him. He shouted at the top of his voice, "What do you want with me, Jesus, Son of the Most High God? In God's name, don't torture me!" For Jesus had said to him, "Come out of this man, you impure spirit!"

I've got some good news. Demons still are afraid of Jesus! And I have some kingdom news for you, too! They are also afraid of you, because you have the kingdom of God inside of you!

Just as Jesus allowed the demons to go into a herd of pigs (vv.12–13), so you can do likewise.

Do you need to change the way you see demons? If you're afraid of demons, like the disciples were, you need to change the way you see. Jesus didn't think they were a big deal at all.

This is normal kingdom living. Just get on with it and cast them out!

Chapter 7: Seeing with Kingdom Eyes - Part 1

> GOOD NEWS! DEMONS ARE STILL AFRAID OF JESUS! THEY ARE ALSO AFRAID OF YOU BECAUSE YOU HAVE THE KINGDOM OF GOD INSIDE YOU.

The demons knew exactly who Jesus was, but the religious leaders did NOT. Instead, they were afraid of Him.

In fact, Mark 5:17 tells us,

> Then the people began to plead with Jesus to leave their region.

The issue has never been about the demons. The whole reason why we have authority over them is for us to demonstrate the kingdom of God here on earth – so other people can SEE Jesus! So others will encounter God, too!

When somebody has been set free by the power of Jesus, they are full of zeal. They are willing to demonstrate the kingdom of God to others in the same way that God has set them free. They make the best kind of witnesses.

Why?

It is impossible for someone to contradict the visible testimony of what God has done for you. This is especially true when everybody in the entire region knows that person!

This is exactly what happened with the man that Jesus set free in the region of the Gerasenes. Everyone knew about the crazy naked man who lived in the graveyard. The miracle of him becoming instantly sane and free was powerful and could not denied.

So instead of allowing the man to go with Him, Jesus turned the man's focus onto telling others what had happened to him when he encountered God. In Mark 5:19–20 we read,

> Jesus did not let him, but said, "Go home to your own people and tell them how much the Lord has done for you, and how he has had mercy on you." So the man went away and began to tell in the Decapolis how much Jesus had done for him. And all the people were amazed.

Never underestimate the power of your testimony. God wants to use you today to set others free so that they can see, too!

Religion will always try to stop others from SEEING God through you.

Religion hates freedom. It wants to keep people blind so they can't see.

Nothing upsets religious leaders more than people being freed from control. This is a challenge because when you see God as He really is, everything changes in your life. Often those who most oppose God's moving are those who supposedly represent Him.

CHAPTER 7: SEEING WITH KINGDOM EYES - PART 1

Lance Wallnau says, "Those on the cutting edge of the last move of God often will persecute the next move of God."

Why? Because the "old wine tastes better" to them.

It only becomes real when a person has a real need. Then religious leaders open up to God, too.

In Mark 5, we are told that Jesus crossed over by boat to the other side of the lake, and a large crowd gathered around him. One of the synagogue leaders named Jairus, came to Jesus and fell at His feet. In verse 22 we read,

> He pleaded earnestly with him, "My little daughter is dying. Please come and put your hands on her so that she will be healed and live."

Notice that he humbled himself before Jesus and Jesus responded to his humility.

God loves humility and hates pride, according to James 4:6!

> "God opposes the proud but shows favor to the humble."

Humility always is the best antidote for religion. James 4:10 says,

> Humble yourselves before the Lord, and he will lift you up.

When confronted by the religious hypocrisy of the Pharisees, Jesus responded, "The greatest among you will be your servant. For those who exalt themselves will be humbled, and those who humble themselves will be exalted" (Matthew 23:11–12).

Humility will always cause you to SEE God! So pursue humility and you will be free from religion.

A humble heart is a pure heart.

Jesus said in Matthew 5:8,

"Blessed are the pure in heart, for they will SEE God."

Having a heart that is right with God will cause you to see God daily. Make sure your heart hungers for Him. Jesus instructs us in Matthew 6:33,

"Seek first his kingdom and his righteousness."

We need to seek it, then we will SEE it!

CHAPTER 8

Seeing with Kingdom Eyes

PART 2

Always expect the unexpected when you begin to SEE God.

When you begin to SEE God's kingdom move in you, the unexpected will happen.

As Jesus was on His way to heal the religious leader's daughter, a large crowd followed Him and tried to get close to Him. Many people reached out to greet Him, but one person reached out in faith, as we read in Mark 5:25–28.

> And a woman was there who had been subject to bleeding for twelve years. She had suffered a great deal under the care of many doctors and had spent all she had, yet instead of

getting better she grew worse. When she heard about Jesus, she came up behind him in the crowd and touched his cloak, because she thought, "If I just touch his clothes, I will be healed."

When she touched Jesus' cloak, the power of God instantly went out of Him.

While the disciples couldn't understand what Jesus was saying, He kept looking around to see who had done it. The woman, knowing that she had been healed, came up to Jesus and fell at His feet. While the disciples couldn't see in the spirit what was happening, Jesus saw the unexpected and embraced it.

It was a miracle on the way to a God-encounter. God always wants miracles to happen, all the time – even when you least expect it.

So you need to expect the unexpected – then don't be surprised when the unexpected happens. It will bring you great joy!

Your seeing becomes stronger in an atmosphere of faith.

When Jesus finally did get to the house of Jairus to heal his daughter, the first thing He did was to make sure there was an atmosphere of faith there. In my book, *Encountering the Supernatural*, a whole chapter teaches you how to create a supernatural atmosphere wherever you go. Jesus practiced this principle. In Mark 5:38–39 we are told,

CHAPTER 8: SEEING WITH KINGDOM EYES - PART 2

When they came to the home of the synagogue leader, Jesus saw a commotion, with people crying and wailing loudly. He went in and said to them, "Why all this commotion and wailing? The child is not dead but asleep."

How did these people respond to the Messiah, savior of the world? *"They laughed at him!"* They laughed at the person who healed all those who were sick and who had delivered so many from demons. This is what religion does. It mocks the presence and power of God.

How did Jesus respond? He kicked them out. He removed the atmosphere of doubt and replaced it with an atmosphere of faith. So, make sure you develop an atmosphere of faith around you for your seeing to be stronger.

There are some people who will never see.

Jesus was careful about who He taught to see God. He was a careful steward of God's anointing, presence and power. And we should be, too! Of course, the little girl immediately stood up and began to walk. Even those who were with Him were completely astonished (Mark 5:42). They still didn't understand who Jesus truly was and how the kingdom of God operated. So this is why Jesus gave strict orders not to tell others.

Why?

The kingdom of God is not for everyone – especially those who oppose Him. I learned a long time ago that some people will not see, even if the miracle is right in front of them. This is what happened to Jesus in Nazareth.

Mark 6:2 reads:

> When the Sabbath came, he began to teach in the synagogue, and many who heard him were amazed.

But instead of being impressed, others were offended, as we continue to read in verses 2 and 3!

> "Where did this man get these things?" they asked. "What's this wisdom that has been given him? What are these remarkable miracles he is performing? Isn't this the carpenter?"

Jesus knew exactly was what was happening. He said to them in verse 4,

> "A prophet is not without honor except in his own town, among his relatives and in his own home."

They were not just denying His incredible teaching, wisdom and authority to heal the sick. They denied that He was from God. Cynicism and offense not only rejected Jesus but also rejected the kingdom of God in their own lives.

Because of their reaction to Jesus, we are told that He couldn't do any miracles there except to heal a few people. Mark 6:6 says,

> He was amazed at their lack of faith.

Faith causes you to see. Doubt will keep you blind. As you continue to see the kingdom of God growing in your life, do not be surprised that some will reject miracles no matter what. For there are some who will never see!

Chapter 8: Seeing with Kingdom Eyes - Part 2

This is sad but true! You need to make sure the unbelief, doubt, offense and lack of honor have no place in your life.

Even Christians can miss out, too! You need to be very careful that you host the kingdom of God well so you will always see!

Authority comes to those who SEE and BELIEVE.

When the disciples saw and believed, Jesus called them together and gave them authority over all disease and spiritual powers. Then He sent them out to others in Mark 6:12–13,

> They went out and preached that people should repent. They drove out many demons and anointed many sick people with oil and healed them.

Now the disciples had to move from seeing Jesus doing signs and wonders to them healing the sick and delivering people from demons. It was their time to do the kingdom – not just see it! As Jesus said in Matthew 10:8,

> "Heal the sick, raise the dead, cleanse those who have leprosy, drive out demons."

Here is the great news. Now it is your turn, too.

Just like the disciples, you have a responsibility because

> "Freely you have received; freely give."

Now it is your TURN to live the kingdom of God and now it is your TIME to live the kingdom of God.

You have to move from seeing and believing to using the authority that you have been given to do what Jesus did here on earth!

It's your responsibility. But He has not left you without authority. You have the authority in the kingdom of God today!

Don't be surprised as the kingdom of God starts to increase in you – you will begin to impact all those you meet. Just recently I spoke to an outlaw biker who was sitting at the table adjacent to me at a coffee shop. He looked mean and intimidating, but as the Lord gave me wisdom, we spoke about deep things in his life for a long time. He was so impacted, he stopped eating altogether and shared many personal things from his past. I was able bring the kingdom of God into His reality that day.

SEE the kingdom of God overflowing out of you even when you least expect it.

When you begin to SEE with His eyes, His presence will overflow onto every person you meet.

Even when you are tired and needing rest, the kingdom of God still flows through you. This happened to Jesus and it will happen to you. Typically, when you're tired the last thing you want to do is to minister the kingdom to others. But the kingdom of God doesn't give us "time off." This was Jesus' experience and will be yours, too.

In Mark 6:30–33, Jesus and His disciples were tired, so they went by boat to rest. But many people saw them leave.

They recognized them and followed them. Instead of sending them away like the disciples wanted to do, Jesus did just the opposite. Mark 6:34 says,

> When Jesus landed and saw a large crowd, he had compassion on them, because they were like sheep without a shepherd. So he began to teach them many things.

The disciples could not see past their own tiredness and inconvenience. They nearly missed out on an incredible miracle.

Why?

God often appears the strongest at the time of the greatest inconvenience! The disciples were tired and hungry, and they wanted Jesus for themselves. But instead, Jesus told them in Mark 6:37,

> "You give them something to eat."

Though the disciples did not react well to this instruction, they had learned to do what Jesus said, and when they did they saw an incredible miracle happen.

In verse 38, He asks,

> "How many loaves do you have?"

Jesus was getting them to SEE what they did have, rather than looking at what they didn't have!

He challenged them to, *"GO and SEE."*

GO and SEE with kingdom of God eyes.

The issue was not the size of the crowd or how much money it would take to buy so much food. They had to SEE with kingdom of God eyes.

Are you beginning to see?

Five thousand people were fed that day with only five loaves of bread and two fish, because Jesus saw the possibilities in an extraordinary miracle needed in extraordinary circumstances.

Even when you are tired and needing rest, miracles will overflow out of you if you are seeing with kingdom eyes.

> EVEN IF YOU ARE TIRED AND NEEDING REST, MIRACLES WILL OVERFLOW OUT OF YOU IF YOU ARE SEEING WITH KINGDOM EYES.

True Kingdom Refreshing

So how do you get refreshed?

Jesus made the disciples get into the boat. But where did Jesus go? He went off by Himself to pray and to spend time being intimate with the Father. In verse 46, we read,

> "After leaving them, he went up on a mountainside to pray."

I remember as a young pastor going away exhausted with my family for our annual vacation. It normally lasted for three weeks, and I enjoyed taking a break from all my pastoral responsibilities to spend time with my wife and young children. But within two or three days of my return from vacation, it was like I had never been away.

Why? I had not learned to refresh my soul. In fact, my devotional life would decrease during the time of vacation. I would "relax" by spending way too much time watching television and movies. I did not know how to relax into God! I sometimes felt I was having a vacation from God, too. The trouble with that scenario was that it was the last thing I needed. I needed to learn to refresh and restore my soul and have a vacation "with" God!

The Bible calls it entering into "God's rest."

The disciples had to learn how to rest God's way and not their soul's way. So Jesus decided to teach them how through a trying experience.

Mark 6:47–50 reads,

> Later that night, the boat was in the middle of the lake, and he was alone on land. He saw the disciples straining at the oars, because the wind was against them. Shortly before dawn he went out to them, walking on the lake. He was about to pass by them, but when they saw him walking on the lake, they thought he was a ghost. They cried out, because they all saw him and were terrified.

What had started out as a holiday quickly began to look like a major problem for them. The last place they needed to be was in the middle of a storm. The truth is – storms happen in the most unlikely times and places in our lives.

When we are in a storm, we need to run *to* Jesus – not away from Him. I hear so many Christians go into the "God, what are You doing to me?" mode instead of hiding themselves in His shelter. That shelter that is carved out in the rock is not meant to be carved out in times of crisis but in times of rest!

Mark 6:51 says,

> Then he climbed into the boat with them, and the wind died down.

We need to let Jesus climb into our boat. The best time to do this is not in the middle of a storm but in our daily desire to SEE Him!

You will SEE more, the deeper you go.

The presence of God will increase in your life the more you SEE Him.

As I was waking up one morning recently, I heard the Lord speak to my spirit,

"Deeper and deeper still."

I realized that the Lord had nailed me! My level of personal encounter had been waning due to busyness of life and the "cares of this world" – even though these cares were largely kingdom of God related. It was time to go deeper!

Chapter 8: Seeing with Kingdom Eyes - Part 2

I saw that the depth of my encounter with God was directly dependent on my willingness for the Lord to dig my soul deeper. I saw that the deeper my soul was dug out by Him, the more room there was for His presence to live inside of me.

I got up and went straight to my place of prayer. I knew I had nowhere else to go but deeper! So that has been my prayer ever since, and it is my prayer for you, too.

If you do not have a heart that is willing to be dug deeper, your soul will get harder even when confronted by the greatest miracles. This is what happened to the religious leaders and even the disciples. And it can happen easily to you and me.

But when you go deeper, there is a greater capacity in you to experience the presence of God. Your intimacy will dramatically increase. Your identity will grow stronger. And God's power will increase in you exponentially. The greater the depth He digs, the more you will see God's kingdom flowing in you and through you to others.

Then you will have kingdom of God seeing!

> WHEN YOU GO DEEPER, THERE IS A GREATER CAPACITY IN YOU TO EXPERIENCE THE PRESENCE OF GOD. YOUR INTIMACY WILL DRAMATICALLY INCREASE. YOUR IDENTITY WILL GROW STRONGER. AND GOD'S POWER WILL INCREASE IN YOU EXPONENTIALLY.

FINAL ENCOURAGEMENT

What I See for You

Let me encourage you. If you have changed the way you see, you have entered a great new season of remarkable miracles and spectacular victories.

Well done! You have chosen to SEE them even before you experience them. Miracles are always for God's glory and for the sake of the kingdom of heaven advancing powerfully here on earth. Now, as long as you keep SEEING with GOD's EYES, these remarkable miracles and spectacular victories will become normal every day life for you.

You have learned how to SEE the kingdom of God. This is because your heart is hungry for more of His kingdom. You have learned to unlock your seeing by seeing from God's perspective, by faith, and you have changed your saying to reflect your new way of seeing!

This kingdom will keep increasing in you because of the different way you now SEE GOD, the way you SEE YOURSELF, the way you SEE OTHERS and the way you SEE the WORLD.

This is because you now truly SEE Him dwelling in you and moving through you.

You are ready for Him to dig in you deeply, so that you will always overflow no matter what place or season of life you are in.

Continue to SEE yourself transformed. As you practice RESTING in this seeing, you will experience life to a whole new level.

Congratulations! You have changed the way you SEE, and everything has changed! You now have a new way of living. Enjoy seeing remarkable miracles and spectacular victories.

You have had a SEEING transformation! I see it! My prayer is that you SEE it, too!

ENDNOTES

Introduction

[1] Definition taken from Dictionary.com (which includes a much more extensive definition).

[2] H.I.M. – Harvest International Ministries

Chapter 1

[1] Strong's Exhaustive Concordance defines *dunamis* as: –force (literally or figuratively); specially, miraculous power (usually by implication, a miracle itself): –ability, abundance, meaning, mighty deed, (worker of) miracle(s), power, strength, violence, mighty (wonderful) work.

[2] "Apostolic Reformation" is best defined by Bill Hamon in his book *Apostles, Prophets and the Coming Moves of God*, Destiny Image Publishers, Inc. 1997.
"There is an emerging Apostolic Movement that will revolutionize the 21st century church. The last generation church will have an Apostolic Reformation that will be as great as the first generation

apostolic movement. The first generation church prophets and apostles laid the foundation of the church. Now the last day Apostolic Reformation will put the final finishing touches on the church. It will also bring revolutionary changes like the protestant movement brought forth in its day. The work of restoration will continue until members of Christ's body are taught, trained, activated and matured in manifesting their membership ministries." (p. 10–11)

Hamon says some perceived revolutionary changes will include:

1. The new Apostolic Reformation will bring about the removal of many "manmade" traditions within the church – for example, the distinction between laity and clergy; pastor's title and role will be redefined.
2. Church cell groups will increase and transition into doing the work of the ministry. The senior pastor will no longer function as the only leader.
3. Believers will begin to manifest the supernatural grace, gifts, and power of God.
4. The leaders in the new Apostolic Reformation will all be fivefold ministers who have progressed from "called to be" to "being commissioned" to their ministry. They will be mature, seasoned men and women of God who have God's heart and mind for His church. The ascension gift of an apostle will be fully restored but apostles will NOT be the only leaders.

The term "Apostolic" has a broader meaning than just for those called to be apostles. Apostolic will include ALL presently restored truth and miraculous ministries with signs, wonders, and miracles by ministers and church members.

[3] *Encountering the Supernatural* by Bruce Lindley. See the last page for more information.

Chapter 4

[1] How to experience the miracle of eternal life!

To become a true believer in Jesus Christ and experience eternal life is not hard at all. It just requires you to be honest with yourself and honest with God and to humbly ask Him to take control of your life from now on. If you have never done that before, here is a simple prayer that will help you do just that:

ADMIT.

"Jesus, I admit that I need you. I cannot save myself and I need a Savior. I realize that my life has been self-centered, and today I want to have You at the center of my life."

Romans 3:23 puts it this way:

All have sinned and fall short of the glory of God.

It is important to realize that you will never be good enough to save yourself. That is why you need a Savior! But there is another important fact here. The glory of God is your way into the supernatural. So to begin your supernatural journey, you need to regain the distance that you have fallen short. Jesus is the only way to do that. Ask Him now.

ASK.

"I ask that You forgive me for all my sins (pause a moment here and be specific). Thank You for dying for me and for taking the consequence of my sin. I ask that You come into my life and take control. I ask that You reveal Your love to me."

God's Word declares this over you today in 1 John 1:9,

If we confess our sins, he is faithful and just and will forgive us our sins and purify us from all unrighteousness.

ACCEPT.

"I accept Your free gift of love, forgiveness, acceptance and eternal life. I was blind but now I see. I accept You as my personal Lord and Savior from today forward in Jesus' name!"

Congratulations. Welcome to the family of God! You are now a Christian – a Christ one!

So now you can step into the lifestyle of transformation.
You get to live what you just began!

Chapter 6

[1] "Restore the Foundations" Ministry
Restoring the Foundations, 2849 Laurel Park Highway
Hendersonville, NC 28739 – www.rtfi.org

[2] *Decree: Third Edition* by Patricia King
XP Publishing, P.O. Box 1017, Maricopa, AZ 85139 USA
www.XPministries.com

Chapter 7

[1] *Encountering the Supernatural* by Bruce Lindley
Australian Apostolic Restore Community (A.A.R.C.)
www.australianarc.org.au

[2] Matthew 10:8,
Heal the sick, raise the dead, cleanse those who have leprosy, drive out demons. Freely you have received; freely give.

Australian Apostolic Resource Community (A.A.R.C.)

A.A.R.C. is an apostolic community of emerging apostles and prophets that exists to build the kingdom of God by walking together in strategic relationships, establishing Fire Houses of Prayer around the Pacific Rim nations and beyond, sending out apostolic and prophetic teams to Australia and the nations, and equip the body of Christ for revival!

A.A.R.C. holds regular supernatural encounter events and also hosts international revival ministries in Australia.

A.A.R.C. is apostolically aligned with a worldwide apostolic network, Harvest International Ministries (H.I.M.)

Go to www.australianarc.org.au/About us
for more information.

Additional Resources by Bruce Lindley

FATHERING A DESTINY – GROWING SPIRITUAL SONS AND DAUGHTERS

This leadership book on the apostolic fathering reformation will give you a next-generation mindset and help you discover your God-destiny as you grow the destiny of others. You will learn how to position in your destiny.

ENCOUNTERING THE SUPERNATURAL

Encountering the Supernatural will take you on a journey to learn how to live in the supernatural on a daily basis as you learn how to build an atmosphere of the supernatural. The supernatural truths that took our spiritual fathers generations to discover are available to you today! Get ready to encounter a whole new realm of the supernatural.

TO ORDER:
Go to the Resources page at
www.australianarc.org.au

To contact Bruce Lindley

to arrange speaking engagements or for additional resources:

Email – admin@australianarc.org.aul

www.ingramcontent.com/pod-product-compliance
Lightning Source LLC
Chambersburg PA
CBHW072054290426
44110CB00014B/1677